# CONTENTS

# WELCOME TO THE WORLD OF INFOGRAPHICS

Using icons, graphics and pictograms, infographics visualise data and information in a whole new way!

**FIND OUT HOW MANY MORE PENGUINS THAN PEOPLE THERE ARE IN ANTARCTICA**

**SEE HOW FAR THE WORLD'S TECTONIC PLATES CAN MOVE IN A YEAR**

**SEE HOW MANY TIMES THE WORLD'S LONGEST COASTLINE CAN STRETCH AROUND THE PLANET**

**COMPARE THE DEPTH OF THE GRAND CANYON TO THE STATUE OF LIBERTY**

# NORTH AMERICA

Stretching from the Arctic to the Caribbean, North America covers 24 million square kilometres, making up about 16 per cent of the world's land area.

NORTH AMERICA

## HIGHEST POINT ON THE CONTINENT

Mt McKinley (Alaska, USA)

**6,194 m**

Mount McKinley

Canada has the world's longest coastline, measuring

**202,080 KM**

... enough to stretch around the world five times.

## How a canyon forms

**1.** Fast-flowing water lifts rocks and mud out of the river bed, creating a channel.

**2.** As more debris is removed, this channel gets deeper. Over time, it may become deep enough to form a steep-sided canyon.

1.

2.

## GRAND CANYON (ARIZONA, USA)

The world's largest land gorge ranges in width from

**180 METRES TO**
**29 KM**

Colorado River

Before the building of the Glen Canyon Dam, the Colorado River, which cut the Grand Canyon, could carry

**500,000 TONNES**

of rocks, mud and debris away every single day. This is the equivalent to the weight of more than four CN Towers – North America's tallest building.

## THE GREAT LAKES

The five Great Lakes in Canada and the USA contain about **23,000 cubic km** of water. That is...

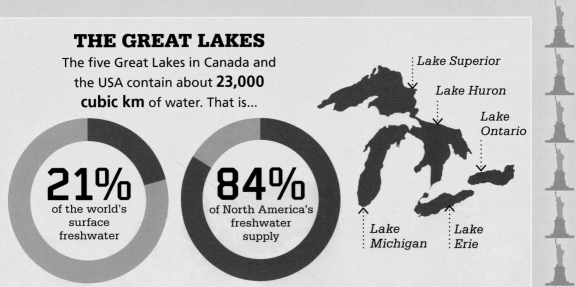

**21%** of the world's surface freshwater

**84%** of North America's freshwater supply

Lake Superior
Lake Huron
Lake Ontario
Lake Michigan
Lake Erie

.... Mississippi River

## Mississippi flow rate

At New Orleans, Louisiana, it is about **16,200** cubic metres **per second...**

... enough to fill **6.5 Olympic swimming pools**

**every second.**

## LOWEST POINT ON THE CONTINENT

Death Valley (California, USA)

86 m below sea level

# RICH COUNTRIES

Much of North America is made up of three large countries – the USA, Canada and Mexico. It also includes Greenland, the world's largest island.

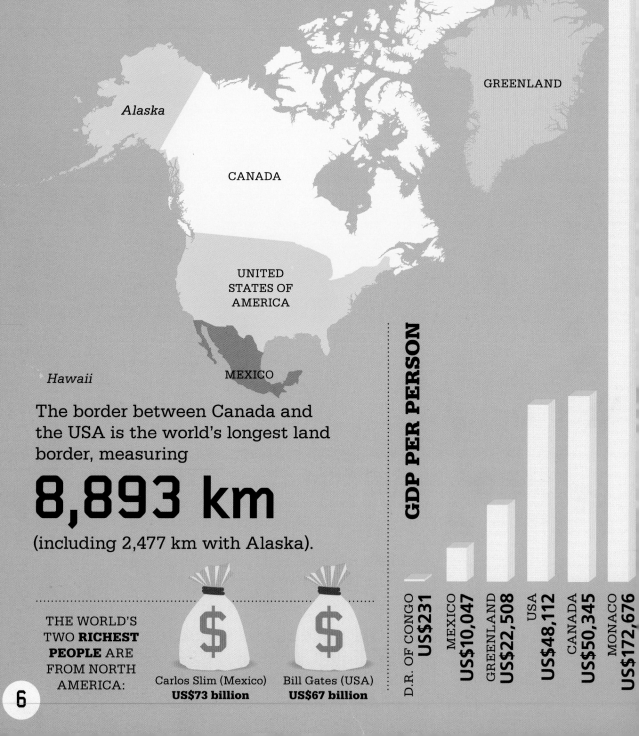

GREENLAND

Alaska

CANADA

UNITED STATES OF AMERICA

Hawaii

MEXICO

The border between Canada and the USA is the world's longest land border, measuring

# 8,893 km

(including 2,477 km with Alaska).

GDP PER PERSON

| D.R. OF CONGO | MEXICO | GREENLAND | USA | CANADA | MONACO |
|---|---|---|---|---|---|
| US$231 | US$10,047 | US$22,508 | US$48,112 | US$50,345 | US$172,676 |

THE WORLD'S TWO **RICHEST PEOPLE** ARE FROM NORTH AMERICA:

Carlos Slim (Mexico)
**US$73 billion**

Bill Gates (USA)
**US$67 billion**

6

THE USA IS A MAJOR FARMING NATION WITH **18%** OF ITS LAND GIVEN OVER TO CROPS, COMPARED TO **12.7%** IN MEXICO, **4.6%** IN CANADA AND LESS THAN **1%** IN GREENLAND.

# 4,760,000

THE NUMBER OF **TRACTORS** IN THE USA – MORE THAN ANY OTHER COUNTRY.

## 16
**PER 1,000 PEOPLE**

CANADA HAS 732,600

## 23
**PER 1,000 PEOPLE**

## PRISONERS
Numbers per 100,000 people

### 715

### 116

---

US WEALTH
**Gross National Income**
(highest in the world)

# US$9,780,000,000,000

BUT THIS WEALTH IS NOT EVENLY DISTRIBUTED

## Poorest 10%
## Wealthiest 10%

### 1.8%
share of income

### 30.5%
share of income

## LIFE EXPECTANCY
average for North America

MEN **73 YEARS**

WOMEN **79 YEARS**

# SOUTH AMERICA

A large part of South America is covered by rainforest. The rainforest around the Amazon River covers more than a third of the continent, or 6 million square kilometres.

The Amazon is the world's second **longest** river, but by far the **largest** by volume. It contains **20%** of all the world's river water.

*Atlantic Ocean*

Manaus

*Amazon River*

At its narrowest point in **Panama,** Central America is just **50 km wide.** The mouth of the Amazon is **320 km wide.**

**SOUTH AMERICA**

## 205,000

Every second, **205,000** cubic metres of water pour out of the Amazon into the Atlantic Ocean.

That is **5 times** more than the world's next largest river, the Congo, and **60 times** more than the longest river, the Nile.

The Andes is about **8,800 km** long and runs through Venezuela, Colombia, Ecuador, Peru, Bolivia, Chile and Argentina.

# RAINFOREST LAYERS

Plants in a rainforest grow to different heights, creating various layers, from the emergents down to the forest floor.

**EMERGENT LAYER**

**CANOPY**

**UNDERSTOREY**

**SHRUB LAYER**

Near Manaus, Brazil, an area of rainforest covering just **175 square metres** (about one-third the area of a football pitch), was found to contain...

**1,652 plants** belonging to **107 species** from **37 families.**

# HIGHEST LAKE IN THE WORLD

**Lake Titcaca** (on the border between Peru and Bolivia)

**3,810 m** above sea level

*Lake Titcaca*

*Iquitos*

*Atacama Desert*

**IQUITOS (PERU)**

**274** cm per year

**ATACAMA DESERT (CHILE)**

**0.01** cm per year

Average rainfall

# RAINFALL

The Atacama Desert in Chile is one of the driest places on Earth.

Some areas have had no rainfall for more than **400 YEARS.**

**50%** The amount that glaciers have shrunk in the Andes due to global warming.

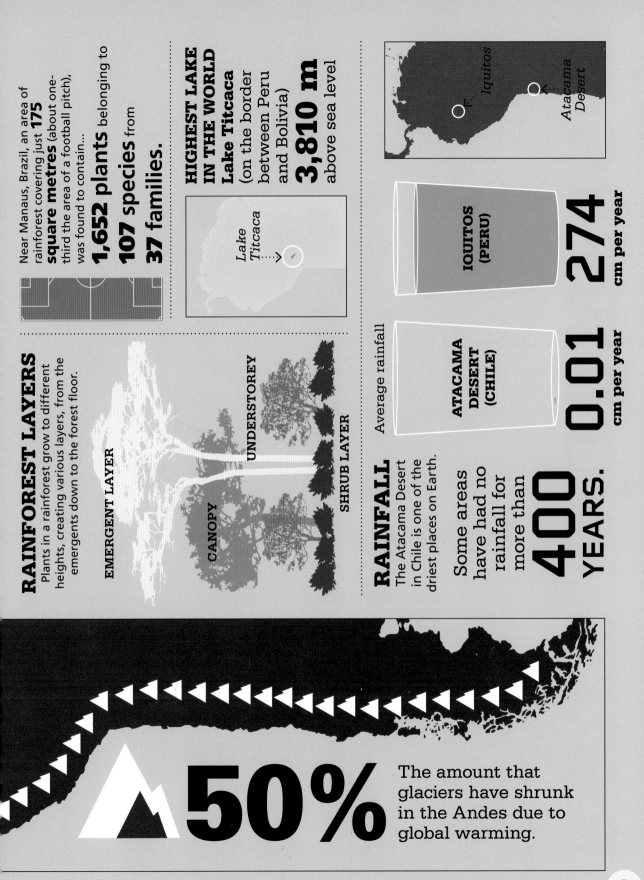

# PEAKS AND RIVERS

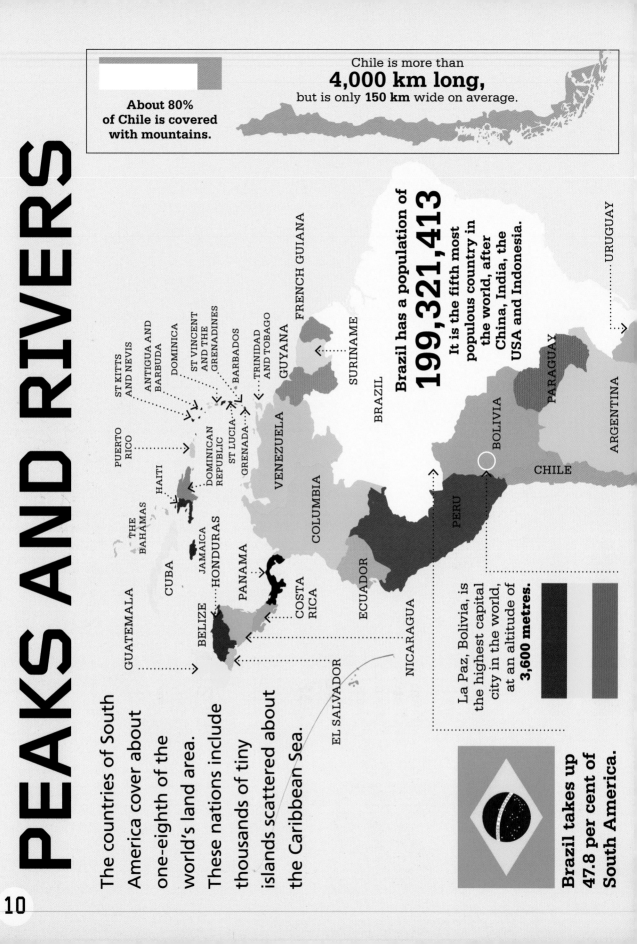

About 80% of Chile is covered with mountains.

Chile is more than **4,000 km long,** but is only **150 km** wide on average.

The countries of South America cover about one-eighth of the world's land area.

These nations include thousands of tiny islands scattered about the Caribbean Sea.

Brazil has a population of **199,321,413**

It is the fifth most populous country in the world, after China, India, the USA and Indonesia.

La Paz, Bolivia, is the highest capital city in the world, at an altitude of **3,600 metres.**

Brazil takes up 47.8 per cent of South America.

GUATEMALA

PUERTO RICO

ST KITTS AND NEVIS

ANTIGUA AND BARBUDA

DOMINICA

ST VINCENT AND THE GRENADINES

BARBADOS

TRINIDAD AND TOBAGO

GUYANA

FRENCH GUIANA

THE BAHAMAS

CUBA

HAITI

DOMINICAN REPUBLIC

ST LUCIA

GRENADA

VENEZUELA

SURINAME

BRAZIL

JAMAICA

HONDURAS

BELIZE

PANAMA

COSTA RICA

COLUMBIA

ECUADOR

PERU

BOLIVIA

PARAGUAY

URUGUAY

ARGENTINA

CHILE

NICARAGUA

EL SALVADOR

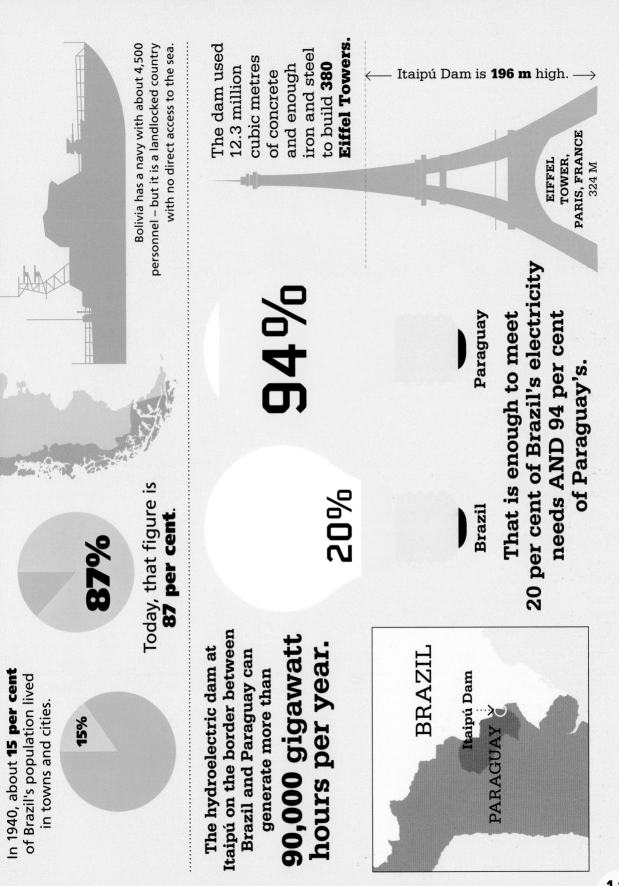

In 1940, about **15 per cent** of Brazil's population lived in towns and cities.

15%

**87%**

Today, that figure is **87 per cent.**

Bolivia has a navy with about 4,500 personnel – but it is a landlocked country with no direct access to the sea.

The dam used 12.3 million cubic metres of concrete and enough iron and steel to build **380 Eiffel Towers.**

← Itaipú Dam is **196 m** high. →

**EIFFEL TOWER, PARIS, FRANCE** 324 M

The hydroelectric dam at Itaipú on the border between Brazil and Paraguay can generate more than **90,000 gigawatt hours per year.**

**94%**

20%

Brazil

Paraguay

**That is enough to meet 20 per cent of Brazil's electricity needs AND 94 per cent of Paraguay's.**

BRAZIL

Itaipú Dam

PARAGUAY

# EUROPE

Europe is the world's second smallest continent. It stretches from the polar waters of the Arctic in the north to the warm Mediterranean Sea in the south.

EUROPE

## MOUNT ETNA

Standing **3,320 m** tall, Etna is Europe's highest active volcano. It measures about **150 km** around its base and covers **1,600 sq km**. That is about **15 per cent** of the island of Sicily, where it is located.

## ICELAND

Iceland sits on the boundary between two of the Earth's tectonic plates (see page 13). As these plates move, red-hot liquid rock pours out, creating volcanoes.

Vatnajökull

Maximum thickness of Vatnajökull **900 m**

The glacier of **Vatnajökull** is the biggest in Europe (by volume) and covers **8 per cent** of Iceland.

The tiny island of Surtsey was created by underwater volcanic eruptions between 1963 and 1967.

**BURJ KHALIFA**
(Dubai) 829.84 M

## LOWEST POINT
Caspian Sea shore (Russia)
**28 m below sea level**

## HIGHEST POINT
Elbrus (Russia)
**5,642 m**

# TECTONIC PLATES

The surface of the Earth is split up into massive plates of rock, called tectonic plates, which move about on the liquid rock beneath. Europe sits on the Eurasian Plate. The place where two plates meet is called a boundary.

| TRANSFORM BOUNDARY | DIVERGENT BOUNDARY | CONVERGENT BOUNDARY |
|---|---|---|
| 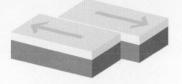 |  |  |
| Two plates rub against each other – there are no transform boundaries in Europe. | Two plates pull apart from each other, as is happening beneath Iceland between the Eurasian Plate and the North American Plate. | Two plates crash into each other, as is happening between the Eurasian Plate and the African Plate. |

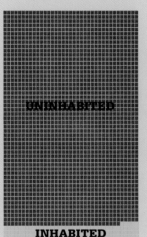

UNINHABITED

INHABITED

**GREECE CONTAINS MORE THAN**

# 2,000 ISLANDS.

**LESS THAN**

# 9% OF THESE ARE INHABITED.

**The coastline of Norway is 100,915 km long, including fjords, indentations and islands.**

**That is enough to stretch 2.5 times around the world.**

# LONGEST RIVER

The longest river in Europe is the Volga. It flows through western Russia for 3,530 km before emptying into the Caspian Sea. Altogether, the river system consists of 151,000 rivers and streams with a total length of

# 570,000 KM.

The distance to the Moon is 384,400 km.

Volga River

Black Sea

Caspian Sea

# LITTLE AND LARGE

Some of the richest countries in the world are found in Europe. Many Europeans can expect to live for a long time thanks to good health care and a high standard of living.

**The tiny republic of San Marino attracts 3.5 million tourists every year.**

**That is more than 110 tourists for every person living there.**

France is the world's most popular tourist destination and more than 76 million visit the country each year.

**But that is only 1.2 tourists for each person living there.**

## LIFE EXPECTANCY

# 89.73 YEARS
– life expectancy of people living in Monaco – the highest in the world.

Male 71

Female 79

Monaco

Average for Europe

FINLAND

NORWAY

SWEDEN

ICELAND

DENMARK

LUXEMBOURG

LITHUANIA

NETHERLANDS

IRELAND

UNITED KINGDOM

GERMANY

POLAN

CZECH REP.

BELGIUM

SLOVA

AUSTRIA

HUNGA

SWITZERLAND

FRANCE

SLOVENIA

ITALY

CROATIA

ANDORRA

SPAIN

PORTUGAL

BOSNIA AND HERZEGOVINA

LIECHTENSTEIN

MONTENEGRO

MONACO

ALBAN

MALTA

MACEDO

# HOT BEVERAGES

## COFFEE

**10.7 KG**

~ 0.7KG

People in Ireland consume just 0.7 kg of coffee beans each year, while those in Norway consume 15 times more.

## TEA

People in the UK consume 2.3 kg of tea leaves each year – 23 times as much as those who live in Italy.

**2.3 KG**

**0.1 KG**

## Largest countries by population

Europe contains just 10 per cent of the world's population.

Russia **143 MILLION**

Germany **82 MILLION**

France **63.5 MILLION**

UK **63 MILLION**

## EUROPEAN UNION

Twenty-eight of the continent's countries have formed a political and economic alliance called the European Union (EU). The Union is the world's biggest importer and exporter of goods.

**IMPORTS**

EU **$2.4 TRILLION**   USA **$2.35 TRILLION**   China **$1.8 TRILLION**

**EXPORTS**

EU **$2.2 TRILLION**   China **$2 TRILLION**   USA **$1.6 TRILLION**

EU member states
EU member states with the Euro as the sole currecy

RUSSIA

ESTONIA

LATVIA

UKRAINE

MOLDOVA

ROMANIA

BULGARIA

TURKEY

EECE

CYPRUS

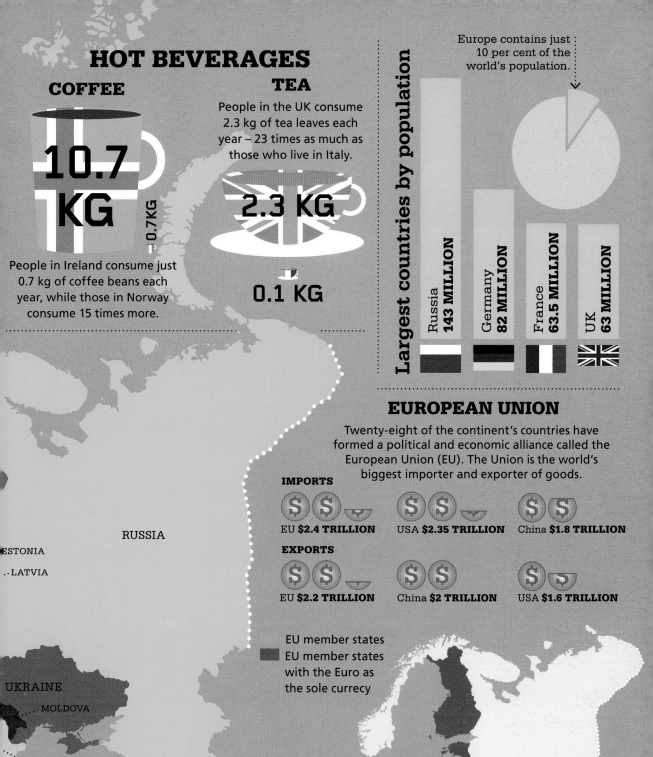

# AFRICA

Africa is a continent of contrasts, where mighty rivers flow through barren deserts and where frozen glaciers sit on the scorching Equator.

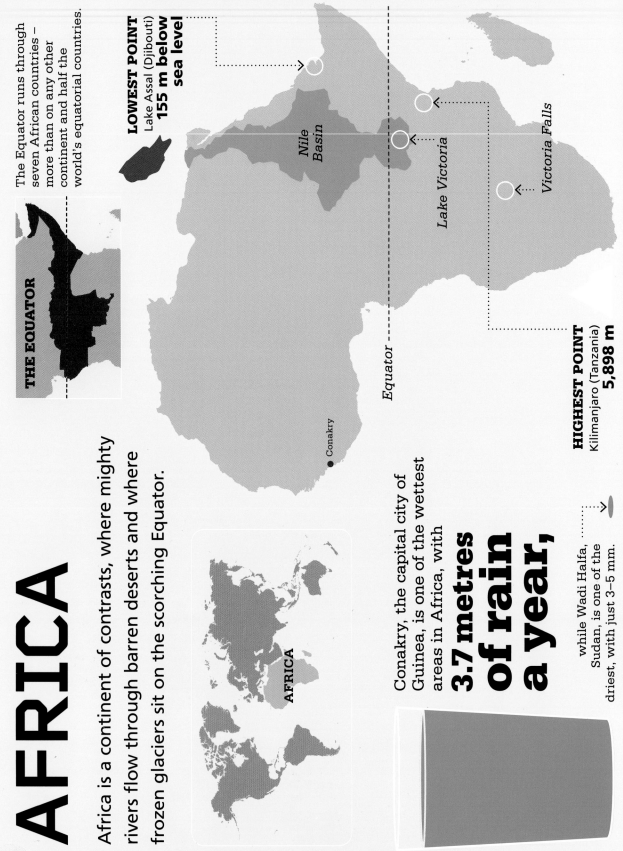

**THE EQUATOR**

The Equator runs through seven African countries – more than on any other continent and half the world's equatorial countries.

**LOWEST POINT**
Lake Assal (Djibouti)
**155 m below sea level**

*Nile Basin*

*Lake Victoria*

*Victoria Falls*

*Equator*

**HIGHEST POINT**
Kilimanjaro (Tanzania)
**5,898 m**

Conakry

AFRICA

Conakry, the capital city of Guinea, is one of the wettest areas in Africa, with

**3.7 metres of rain a year,**

while Wadi Halfa, Sudan, is one of the driest, with just 3–5 mm.

## THE NILE

The Nile is the world's longest river. It is

# 6,650 km

in length.

*Nile River*

Its river basin covers about 10% of the continent.

**10%**

NETHERLANDS

BELGIUM

FRANCE

Over the last 50 years, the Sahara has increased in size by **650,000 sq km** – larger than France, Belgium and the Netherlands combined.

## LARGEST LAKE

Africa's largest lake is Lake Victoria on the borders of Uganda, Kenya and Tanzania. It covers

# 69,484 SQ KM

### LARGEST WATERFALL

Victoria Falls is Africa's largest waterfall. On average, some 1,088 cubic metres of water flow over the falls each second – which could fill Wembley Stadium (UK) in **an hour.**

**WEMBLEY STADIUM**

*Lake Victoria*

*Victoria Falls*

**5.8%**
Deforestation

**57.8%**
Overgrazing

Causes of desertification in Africa

**19.5%**
Agricultural activities

**16.9%**
Overexploitation of vegetation for domestic use

### HOW DESERTS FORM

The transformation of fertile land into desert – known as desertification – happens in a number of ways. These include overgrazing by farm animals, cutting down forest, poor farming practices and the overuse of plants for home use, such as fuel.

The Sahara Desert covers about

# 8,600,000 sq km

which is about 28 per cent of the entire continent. It is also **bigger than Australia.**

*Sahara*

# CHANGING BORDERS

The African continent contains more than 50 countries. The exact number frequently changes as some areas are disputed by two or more countries, while new countries emerge from civil wars.

TUNISIA

MOROCCO

ALGERIA

WESTERN SAHARA

MAURITANIA

MALI

NIGER

CAPE VERDE

BURKINA FASO

GUINEA

THE GAMBIA

SIERRA LEONE

IVORY COAST

GHANA

BENIN

NIGERIA

Lagos

GUINEA-BISSAU

LIBERIA

TOGO

CAMEROON

SÃO TOMÉ AND PRÍNCIPE

EQUATORIAL GUINEA

GABON

CONGO

NAMIBIA

## LIFE EXPECTANCY

## 38.76 YEARS

the life expectancy of people living in Angola – the lowest in the world.

Male 52

Female 56

Angola

Average for Africa

The most populous nation in Africa is **Nigeria**. It has a population of more than **162 million** (about 16.6 per cent of the continent's entire population).

## YOUNGEST COUNTRY IN THE WORLD

**South Sudan**
Declared a sovereign state on

**9 JULY 2011**

**The Seychelles** is Africa's smallest country. It is made up of 115 islands in the Indian Ocean. These have a total area of 455 sq km (about 2.5 times the size of Washington, DC), and a population of

## 90,000.

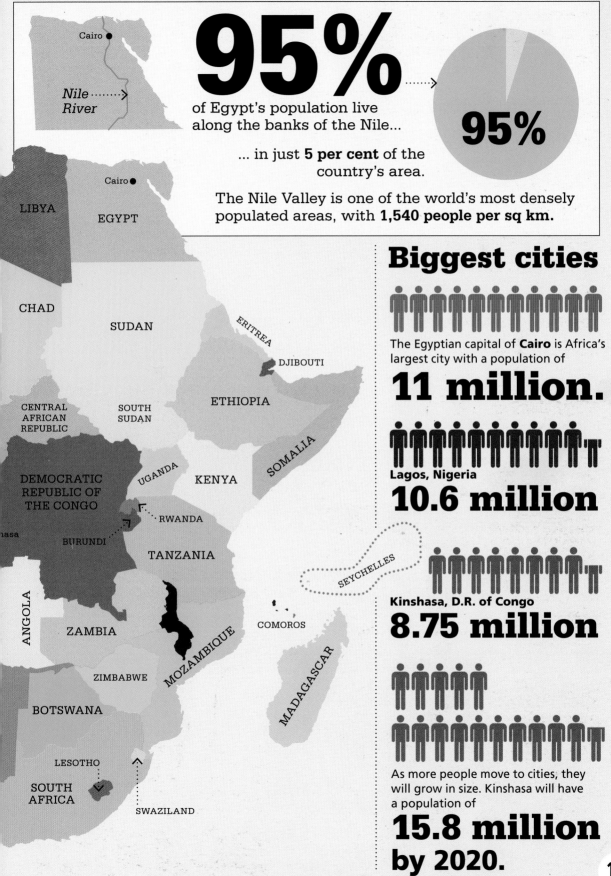

# 95%

of Egypt's population live along the banks of the Nile...

95%

... in just **5 per cent** of the country's area.

The Nile Valley is one of the world's most densely populated areas, with **1,540 people per sq km.**

Cairo
Nile River

LIBYA
Cairo
EGYPT
CHAD
SUDAN
ERITREA
DJIBOUTI
CENTRAL AFRICAN REPUBLIC
SOUTH SUDAN
ETHIOPIA
DEMOCRATIC REPUBLIC OF THE CONGO
UGANDA
KENYA
SOMALIA
RWANDA
BURUNDI
TANZANIA
SEYCHELLES
ANGOLA
ZAMBIA
COMOROS
MOZAMBIQUE
MADAGASCAR
ZIMBABWE
BOTSWANA
LESOTHO
SOUTH AFRICA
SWAZILAND
hasa

## Biggest cities

The Egyptian capital of **Cairo** is Africa's largest city with a population of

# 11 million.

**Lagos, Nigeria**

# 10.6 million

**Kinshasa, D.R. of Congo**

# 8.75 million

As more people move to cities, they will grow in size. Kinshasa will have a population of

# 15.8 million
by 2020.

# ASIA

The world's largest continent stretches from the Mediterranean in the west to the Pacific in the east. It is filled with enormous forests, huge grassy plains and the planet's highest peaks.

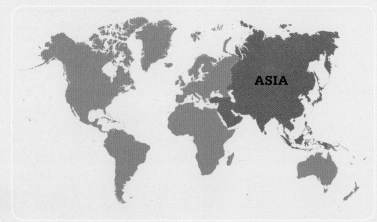

ASIA

**CHINA** is the biggest country in Asia. It covers 9,572,900 sq km...

... about **21.5%** of the entire continent.

Asia (including the Asian part of Russia) makes up about one-third of the planet's land surface. That is

# 44,614,000 SQ KM

## HIGHEST AND LOWEST POINTS IN ASIA

**LOWEST POINT**
Dead Sea
(Israel and Jordan)
**400 m below sea level**

*Dead sea*

**HIGHEST POINT**
Mount Everest
(Nepal and China)
**8,850 m**

## DECLINE OF THE ARAL SEA

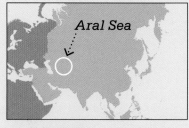

*Aral Sea*

**1957**      **2000**

The diversion of the rivers that used to feed the Aral Sea have caused it to shrink. At the current rate, it will disappear completely by 2020.

# 20-25 MILLION YEARS

The age of Lake Baikal, Russia, the world's oldest freshwater lake.

Lake Baikal is the largest freshwater lake by volume and holds 20 per cent of the Earth's surface freshwater.

**20%**

**23,000 CUBIC KM OF WATER**

*Lake Baikal*

**1,642 M DEEP**

EIFFEL TOWER 324 M

# FORMING THE HIMALAYAS

The world's highest mountain range, the Himalayas, was formed by the movement of the tectonic plates that make up the Earth's crust.

**Around 70 million years ago, the Indian plate started pushing into the Eurasian plate.**

*Converging plates*

*Himalayas*

*Eurasian Plate*

*Eurasian Plate...*   *Sea...*   *...Indian Plate*

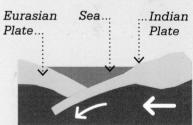

The sea between the two plates grew smaller and the sea floor was pushed up.

*......Himalayas*

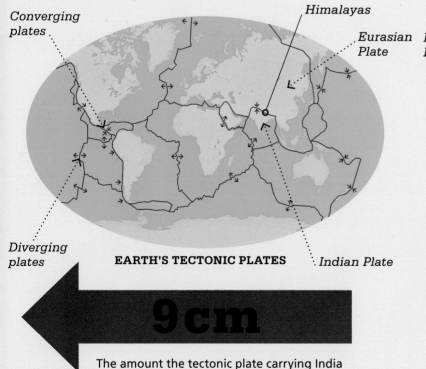

*Diverging plates*

**EARTH'S TECTONIC PLATES**

*: Indian Plate*

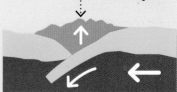

**9cm**

The amount the tectonic plate carrying India pushes into the Asian tectonic plate each year.

Eventually, the rocks of the sea floor were pushed up to form the Himalayas.

# SUPER STATES

The countries of Asia include some of the largest in the world. They have enormous populations producing and consuming vast amounts of food and other products.

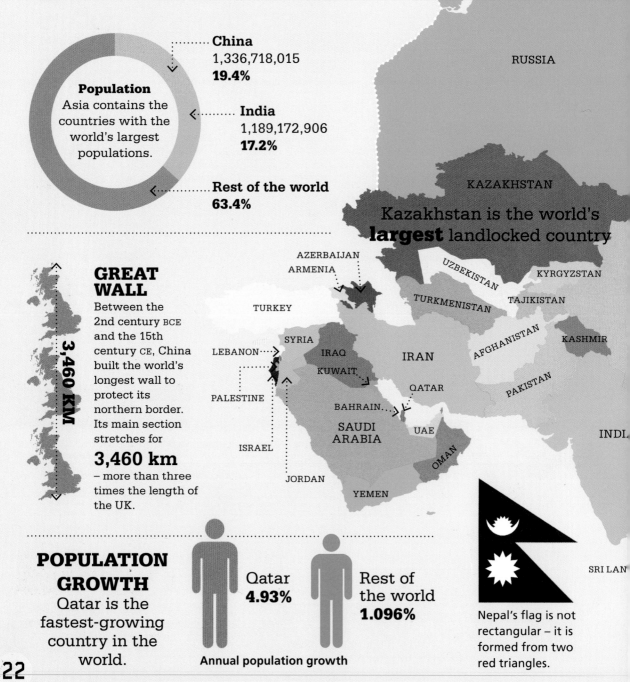

**Population**
Asia contains the countries with the world's largest populations.

**China**
1,336,718,015
**19.4%**

**India**
1,189,172,906
**17.2%**

**Rest of the world**
**63.4%**

## GREAT WALL

Between the 2nd century BCE and the 15th century CE, China built the world's longest wall to protect its northern border. Its main section stretches for

**3,460 km**

– more than three times the length of the UK.

**3,460 KM**

Kazakhstan is the world's **largest** landlocked country

RUSSIA

KAZAKHSTAN

AZERBAIJAN
ARMENIA
UZBEKISTAN
KYRGYZSTAN
TURKMENISTAN
TAJIKISTAN
TURKEY
SYRIA
AFGHANISTAN
KASHMIR
LEBANON
IRAQ
IRAN
KUWAIT
PALESTINE
QATAR
PAKISTAN
BAHRAIN
ISRAEL
SAUDI
ARABIA
UAE
INDIA
JORDAN
OMAN
YEMEN
SRI LAN

## POPULATION GROWTH

Qatar is the fastest-growing country in the world.

Qatar
**4.93%**

Rest of the world
**1.096%**

**Annual population growth**

Nepal's flag is not rectangular – it is formed from two red triangles.

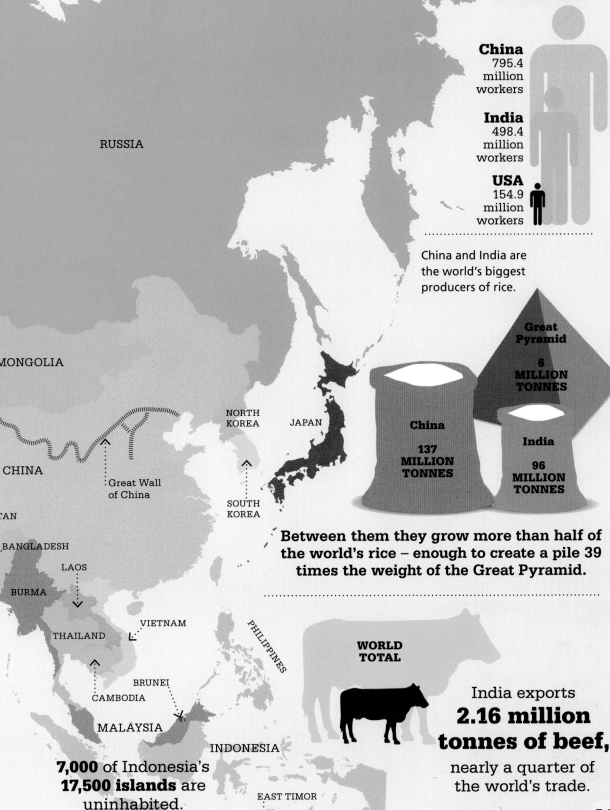

## ASIA'S WORKFORCE

**China**
795.4 million workers

**India**
498.4 million workers

**USA**
154.9 million workers

China and India are the world's biggest producers of rice.

**Great Pyramid**
6 MILLION TONNES

**China**
137 MILLION TONNES

**India**
96 MILLION TONNES

**Between them they grow more than half of the world's rice – enough to create a pile 39 times the weight of the Great Pyramid.**

RUSSIA

MONGOLIA

NORTH KOREA

JAPAN

CHINA

Great Wall of China

SOUTH KOREA

BHUTAN

BANGLADESH

LAOS

BURMA

THAILAND

VIETNAM

PHILIPPINES

CAMBODIA

BRUNEI

MALAYSIA

INDONESIA

EAST TIMOR

**WORLD TOTAL**

India exports
**2.16 million tonnes of beef,**
nearly a quarter of the world's trade.

**7,000** of Indonesia's **17,500 islands** are uninhabited.

23

# AUSTRALIA AND OCEANIA

The region of Oceania is made up of the countries of Australia, New Zealand and more than a dozen nations found throughout the Pacific Ocean.

**PAPUA NEW GUINEA**
462,840 sq km
5.4%

**NEW ZEALAND**
270,692 sq km
3.2%

**THE REST**
89,268 sq km
1.1%

**HIGHEST POINT**
Mt Wilhelm, Papua New Guinea
**4,509 m**

**AUSTRALIA**
7,702,501 sq km
90.3%

The largest country in Oceania is Australia, which covers 7,702,501 sq km.

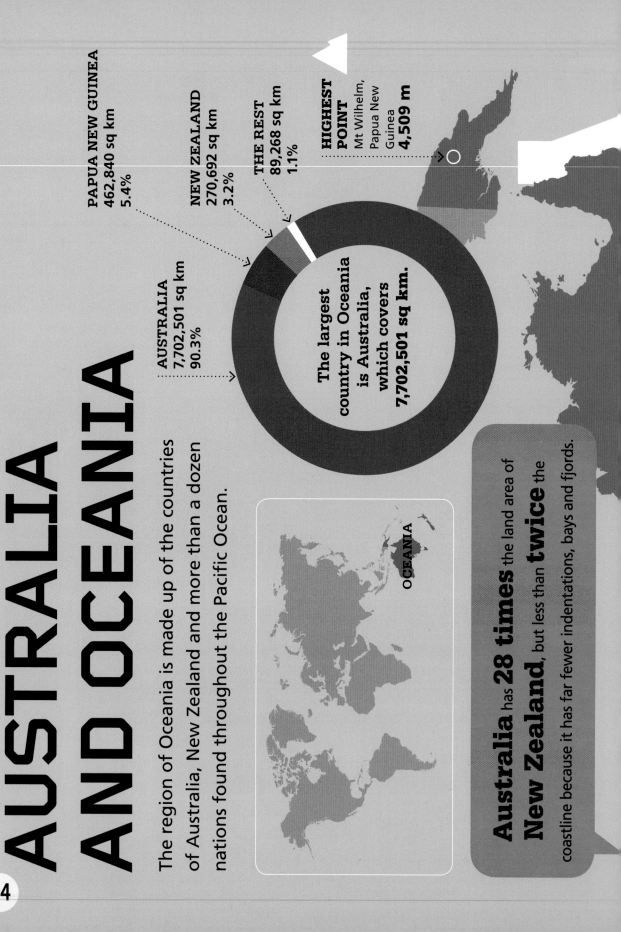

OCEANIA

**Australia** has **28 times** the land area of **New Zealand**, but less than **twice** the coastline because it has far fewer indentations, bays and fjords.

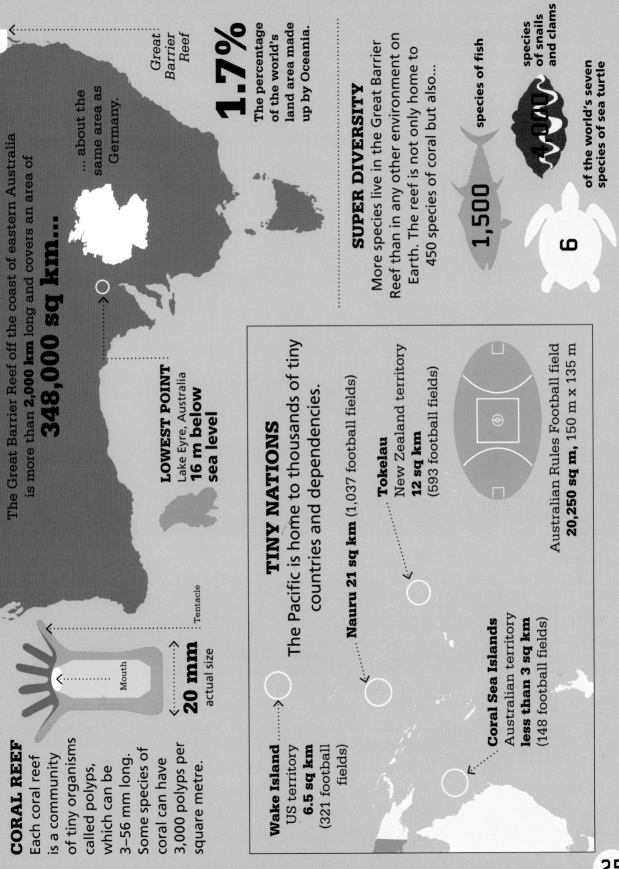

**CORAL REEF**

Each coral reef is a community of tiny organisms called polyps, which can be 3–56 mm long. Some species of coral can have 3,000 polyps per square metre.

Mouth

Tentacle

**20 mm** actual size

The Great Barrier Reef off the coast of eastern Australia is more than **2,000 km** long and covers an area of

**348,000 sq km...**

... about the same area as Germany.

*Great Barrier Reef*

**1.7%**

The percentage of the world's land area made up by Oceania.

**LOWEST POINT**

Lake Eyre, Australia **16 m below sea level**

**SUPER DIVERSITY**

More species live in the Great Barrier Reef than in any other environment on Earth. The reef is not only home to 450 species of coral but also...

**1,500** species of fish

**4,000** species of snails and clams

**6** of the world's seven species of sea turtle

**TINY NATIONS**

The Pacific is home to thousands of tiny countries and dependencies.

**Nauru 21 sq km** (1,037 football fields)

**Tokelau**
New Zealand territory
**12 sq km**
(593 football fields)

**Wake Island**
US territory
**6.5 sq km**
(321 football fields)

**Coral Sea Islands**
Australian territory
**less than 3 sq km**
(148 football fields)

Australian Rules Football field
**20,250 sq m**, 150 m x 135 m

# PACIFIC PARADISE

The countries of Oceania are scattered over more than 10,000 islands that lie across thte millions of square kilometres of the Pacific Ocean.

GUAM

PALAU

Yap

MICRONESIA

PAPUA NEW GUINEA

SOLO

## 700

The number of languages spoken in the country of Papua New Guinea. It has a population of just over **6 million.**

AUSTRALIA

REST OF THE CONTINENT

AUSTRALIA

**39%**

**61%**

LARGEST CITY
Sydney (Australia)
**4,336,374**

About 37 million people inhabit the islands and countries of Oceania, 22,651,000 of which live in Australia alone.

NEW ZEALAN

## POPULATION GROWTH

The Cook Islands in the Pacific has the slowest growing population. In fact it is shrinking at a rate of -3.14%.

**Annual population growth**

Cook Islands
**-3.14%**

Rest of the world
**1.096%**

MARSHALL ISLANDS

KIRIBATI

NAURU

ANDS

TUVALU

TOKELAU

WESTERN SAMOA

VANUATU

FIJI

NIUE

NEW CALEDONIA

AMERICAN SAMOA

COOK ISLANDS

FRENCH POLYNESIA

TONGA

Total land area of Pacific islands
**822,800 sq km**

**0.5%**

**165,200,000 sq km**
Total area of the Pacific Ocean

**13%**
of New Zealand's electricity is produced by geothermal energy, most of it from the Taupo Volcanic Zone.

Oceania lies next to the

# International Date Line,

which runs through the Pacific from the North Pole to the South Pole. The date changes by one day either side of the International Date Line. It is not a straight line, but passes around island groups, so they all have the same date.

Taupo Volcano

**MOST SOUTHERLY CAPITAL CITY**
Wellington, New Zealand
**41°17'S**

Hundreds of years ago, the tiny Pacific island of **Yap** used huge, doughnut shaped stones as money.

**The largest are 3.5 m across, 0.5 m thick and can weigh 4 tonnes.**

**3.5 M**

**1.8 M**

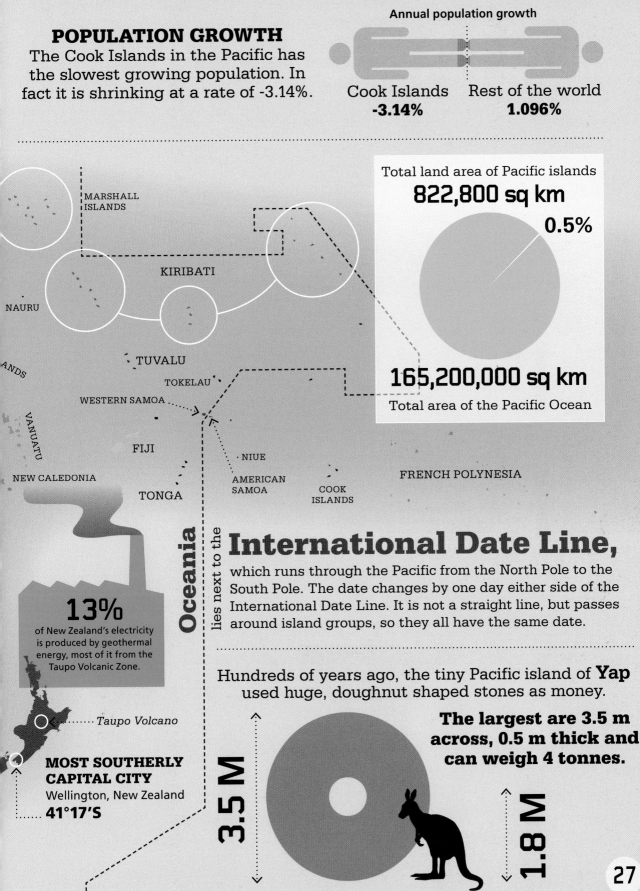

27

# ANTARCTICA

Because of the Earth's tilt, the world's most southerly and coldest continent experiences six months of daylight followed by six months of darkness.

Antarctica contains no countries, but several areas are claimed and controlled by other nations, including the UK, Norway, Australia, New Zealand, France, Chile and Argentina.

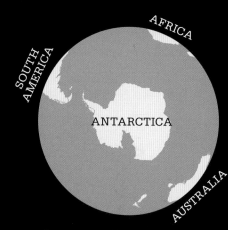

SOUTH AMERICA

AFRICA

ANTARCTICA

AUSTRALIA

**Antarctica covers 14.2 million sq km** – nearly twice the area of Australia. Only 280,000 sq km of this is not covered with ice.

2% barren rock

**98% covered in ice**

2,450 m

829.84 m

**HIGHEST POINT**
Vinson Massif
**4,697 m**

Antarctica's ice sheet contains 29 million cubic km of ice – 90 per cent of the world's total glacial ice. **It has an average thickness of 2,450 m – three times the height of the Burj Khalifa (Dubai), the tallest building in the world to date.**

# TEMPERATURE RANGES

Antarctica is the world's coldest place. Average temperatures range from just +1°C near the coast during summer, to a freezing -80°C and less in winter.

## POPULATION OF ANTARCTICA

The population of Antarctica increases by 500 per cent during the milder summer months of October to February, when it is easier to travel there.

**WINTER**
1,000 people

**SUMMER**
5,000 people

........ **SOUTH POLE**

**VOSTOK STATION**
**-89.2°C**
Lowest recorded temperature on Earth

## COMPARISON BETWEEN ANTARCTIC POPULATIONS

**5,000**
People

**595,000**
Emperor penguins

**100°C**
Boiling point of water

**56.7°C**
Highest recorded temperature on Earth

**37°C**
Human body temperature

**0°C**

**-10°C**
Average coastal temperature in Antarctica

**-60°C**
Average inland elevated temperature in Antarctica

**-67.7°C**
Lowest recorded temperature in Oimaykon, Russia

**-89.2°C**
Lowest recorded temperature on Earth

At its peak during the 2007–2008 season, **46,265 tourists** visited Antarctica, compared to 76 million who visited France, the world's most popular tourist destination.

# GLOSSARY

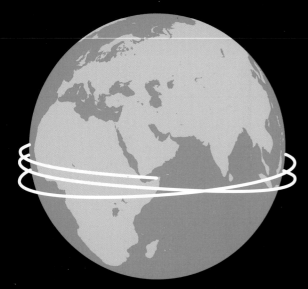

### canopy
The layer of interconnecting treetops in a rainforest, high above the forest floor, but just below the emergents.

### canyon
A type of gorge or chasm with very steep sides cut into the landscape by flowing water – usually a river.

### dependency
Territories that are governed by – or dependent on – other countries.

### desertification
The process by which fertile land gradually becomes infertile and turns into barren desert.

### emergent
The highest trees in a rainforest that 'emerge' from the top of the canopy.

### Equator
An imaginary line running horizontally around the centre of the Earth. It is the line of 0° latitude.

### GDP
Gross domestic product – the total value of all the goods and services produced by a nation.

### geothermal
Relating to heat created beneath the Earth's surface. Geothermal energy can be used to heat water to produce steam and produce electricity.

### gigawatt hours
A large unit of energy – the amount of power (in gigawatts, the equivalent of 1,000 megawatts or 1 billion watts) produced every hour.

### glacier
A thick body of ice that moves very slowly down a mountain valley.

### language
A common form of speech and writing shared by a people, usually living in the same country.

# global warming

An increase in the average temperature of the Earth's atmosphere, which may be caused by man-made pollution.

# gross national income

The total value of goods and services produced by a nation (the Gross Domestic Product), plus any revenue received from foreign countries, minus any payments made to foreign countries.

# hydroelectric dam

A large dam built across a river, which uses the controlled flow of water through the dam to produce electricity.

# tectonic plates

The enormous sheets of rock that make up the Earth's surface.

# International Date Line

An imaginary line running through the Pacific Ocean from the North Pole to the South Pole. The date changes by one day either side of the line. It is the line of 180° longitude.

# landlocked

A country that does not have a border with the sea, but is surrounded on all sides by other countries.

# life expectancy

The average age to which a person can expect to live.

# republic

A country that is ruled by a president rather than a monarch. The president is usually voted for by the people of the country.

# river basin

The area of land that feeds a river and its tributaries (small rivers that flow into the main river) with water.

# understorey

The area in a rainforest beneath the canopy that receives very little sunlight.

## Websites

**MORE INFO:**
**www.timeforkids.com/around-the-world**
Online magazines celebrating the culture, people, landmarks and geography of countries with photographs, diagrams and maps.

**kids.nationalgeographic.co.uk/kids/places/**
Information on the countries of the world, with lots of games and online activities.

**news.bbc.co.uk/1/hi/country_profiles/default.stm**
Searchable database of guides and profiles to the countries of the world with audio and video clips from the BBC archives.

**MORE GRAPHICS:**
**www.visualinformation.info**
A website that contains a whole host of infographic material on subjects as diverse as natural history, science, sport and computer games.

**www.coolinfographics.com**
A collection of infographics and data visualisations from other online resources, magazines and newspapers.

**www.dailyinfographic.com**
A comprehensive collection of infographics on an enormous range of topics that is updated every single day!

# INDEX

# ACKNOWLEDGEMENTS

Published in paperback in 2014 by Wayland
Copyright © Wayland 2014

Wayland
338 Euston Road
London NW1 3BH

Wayland Australia
Level 17/207 Kent Street
Sydney NSW 2000

All rights reserved.
Senior editor: Julia Adams

Produced by Tall Tree Ltd
Editors: Jon Richards and Joe Fullman
Designer: Ed Simkins
Consultant: Kim Bryan

Dewey classification: 910

ISBN: 9780750283069

Printed in Malaysia
10 9 8 7 6 5 4 3 2 1

Wayland is a division of Hachette
Children's Books, an Hachette UK company.
www.hachette.co.uk

The website addresses (URLs) included in this
book were valid at the time of going to press.
However, because of the nature of the Internet,
it is possible that some addresses may have
changed, or sites may have changed or closed
down, since publication. While the author and
Publisher regret any inconvenience this may
cause the readers, no responsibility for any such
changes can be accepted by either the author
or the Publisher.